Minimum Wage, Maximum Sentence

Special thanks to Christopher Frappier for teaching me about the inequalities of the criminal justice system. And to all the inmates who shared their stories with me.

Table of Contents

Photo by Ashley Aubert

Introduction

One out of every 33 Americans is currently incarcerated. The United States holds more people in correctional facilities than any other country in the world. Shown in figure 1 is the dramatic increase in the incarcerated population overall, this includes people currently on parole and probation. The rate of incarceration has increased dramatically since the 1970's.

Who are these people most of us only hear of or see on TV? Popular culture and the media have created an image of the men and women behind bars with tattoos covering 35 percent of their bodies, dark eyes with nothing behind them, and an attraction to causing harm to those in their paths. We fear the day they will be released back into our safe communities, what are we supposed to do?

Unfortunately this is the brutal reality of how the individuals that make up our prison system are portrayed whether in the media or in our society. Most inmates are not covered in tattoos, some don't even have tattoos. The majority of inmates are also incarcerated for nonviolent offenses. In reality, these individuals are conscious of the choices they've made, accepting of the reality they have to wake up to each morning, and are avid protectors of the people they love and care about the most.

So why are these seemingly "normal" people currently locked behind bars, supervised twenty four hours a day? The answer is rooted in socioeconomic status, the economic way of life that you are born into. From the day a child is born into a low economic level in society, they will be faced with daily struggles unknown to those more fortunate. Once that individual is arrested, their socioeconomic level becomes a permanent stain. It affects their inability to afford private legal representation, receive fair sentencing, and successfully transfer back to their community once they are released. In American society money is no longer solely about corporations and politics. It has seeped its way into the lives of men and woman who have become a victim of what has proven too often, to be a discriminatory justice system.

America prides itself on being fair and equal and although it may try to deliver healthcare or marriage rights to all individuals, it falls far behind when it comes to individuals facing incarceration. How is a country that set its roots on opportunity and the "chance to make it big" discriminating against its citizens with less money? Poverty is everywhere in America, and yes there are charities, but what about the poor who are arrested and sentenced to years in prison for stealing something so they could feed their family? Where is the justice and fair and equal treatment for these individuals?

Where is the charity for those who are addicted to drugs and cannot afford treatment so they steal or sell their bodies to feed their illness? We don't hear about these people because society has labeled them as convicts, criminals, and "bad people." In reality they are like you and me, but their lives present a daily struggle to survive and the light at the end of the tunnel for so many of us, is a dimly lit prison cell for so many of them.

In my research I investigate a progression that occurs in the life of someone from a low-economic background. From the first time they get arrested money is a factor, during their court process money is a factor. Once they are released from prison; money is once again a factor. For these people that simply don't have the money, the criminal justice system is a vicious circle with no "optional" entrance and no exit.

Just how early does money affect an individual's likelihood of being incarcerated? And how strong is this effect? Is there really an answer to why a majority of those incarcerated are poor? In the interviews I have conducted, professionals from the criminal justice system have identified numerous factors in society and the criminal justice system that are set up to make the poor fail. Inmates have told me stories of tragic childhoods and their first arrest that led them down a path of constant involvement in the criminal system with no opportunity of getting out.

From a young age, my fascination with jails and inmates has allowed me to visit jails, speak with inmates, and question just what it is that causes someone to commit a crime? In the summer of 2011 I interned at the Public Defenders office in Burlington, Vermont. It is here that I was introduced to an issue in our society rarely mentioned and frequently ignored.

After speaking with inmates in various Vermont facilities I began to notice a pattern of socioeconomic factors that played into the causes of the crime, reasons for committing the crime, and the repercussions that lead to repeat offenses. I wrote this book to dispel the popular opinions on inmates and to investigate a "hidden" form of discrimination that affects so many. And the lack of initiatives to create a solution.

Total Corrections Population

Incarcerated, Reentry, Intermediate Sanctions, Parole, & Probation

Figure 1

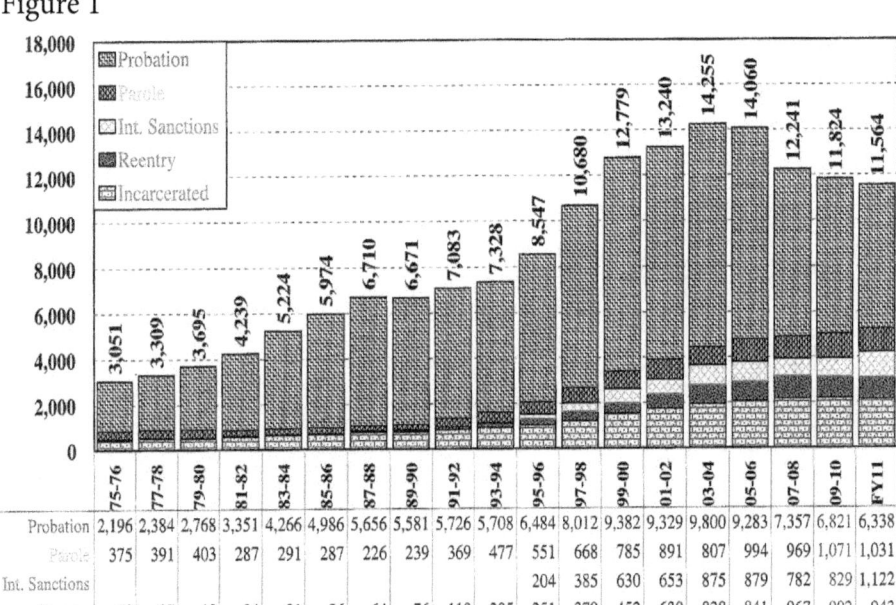

	75-76	77-78	79-80	81-82	83-84	85-86	87-88	89-90	91-92	93-94	95-96	97-98	99-00	01-02	03-04	05-06	07-08	09-10	FY11
Probation	2,196	2,384	2,768	3,351	4,266	4,986	5,656	5,581	5,726	5,708	6,484	8,012	9,382	9,329	9,800	9,283	7,357	6,821	6,338
Parole	375	391	403	287	291	287	226	239	369	477	551	668	785	891	807	994	969	1,071	1,031
Int. Sanctions											204	385	630	653	875	879	782	829	1,122
Reentry	50	27	18	24	31	26	64	76	119	205	251	379	452	630	828	841	967	902	943
Incarcerated	430	507	506	577	636	675	764	775	869	938	1,057	1,236	1,530	1,737	1,945	2,063	2,166	2,201	2,130

Biennum (Fiscal) Years

Source: Vermont Dept of Corrections (VTDOC) Population Statistics (Popstat) and Snapshot databases, includes inmates housed out-of-state.

Note: Fiscal Year averages for incarcerated, Reentry and Intermediate Sanctions: Point-in-Time numbers for Probation and Parole prior to FY2011 (thereafter FY averages.) For compatibility to earlier years, persons with multiple simultaneous statuses are counted under all applicable statuses.

*Reproduced with permission from the Vermont Department of Corrections

Chapter 1

Born into Poverty in an Age of Socioeconomic Discrimination

Photo by Ashley Aubert

In a statistical analysis by John Irwin conducted in 1992 one hundred arrests across America were narrowed down to the different crimes committed. On average 30 crimes out of one hundred were "narcotics violations" which include any prohibited substances, followed by fourteen out of a hundred "burglaries."The crimes were then narrowed down to categories of the individuals that had committed the crimes.

"Petty hustlers "described as the most likely to be arrested, spend most of their days on the streets trying to sell small quantities of marijuana or a fake substitute.(Irwin, John. The Jail: Managing the Underclass in American Society. Berkeley: University of California, 1985. Print.) They constituted 28 out of the one hundred arrested. These individuals are usually from low income neighborhoods and are more likely to be arrested. What separates these crimes from others is their frequency and how they are generally seen as the most annoying to the public, but are never the most violent or severe.

In Vermont the most common crime committed by men is DUI3, the number three represents a third time being charged with the crime. For women the most common crime is DUI2. When it comes to individuals from lower socioeconomic status, the majority of the crimes they commit are related to an absence of money. Stealing to resell items is a reoccurring crime I was told of in my interviews with the inmates. For Michael Francis, stealing was a way of surviving. After his parents split up when he was 13 and he was left alone with no other way to survive.

Francis says he turned to stealing "to survive, to eat, for shelter" he said. Still coping with the separation of his parents Francis says he knew stealing was his only option. "I'm not one to start trouble" says Francis. Drinking and an addiction to opiates have led Francis to over twenty years of incarceration at different times in his life.

When I met 27 year old Adam Jankowski he was the only African American inmate I had spoken to. Being the second most homogenous state after Maine, Vermont is primarily white. As shown in figure 2 the majority of individuals currently incarcerated are white with only a small percent being Black. The majority of black inmates in Vermont facilities are from out of state.

Serving time for "escaping with possession of stolen property" Jankowski described his childhood in Buffalo New York and the sudden change that caused him to get arrested when he was just 15. Like Francis, Jankowski was never a trouble maker before his mother

Racial Composition under Field Supervision

Figure 2

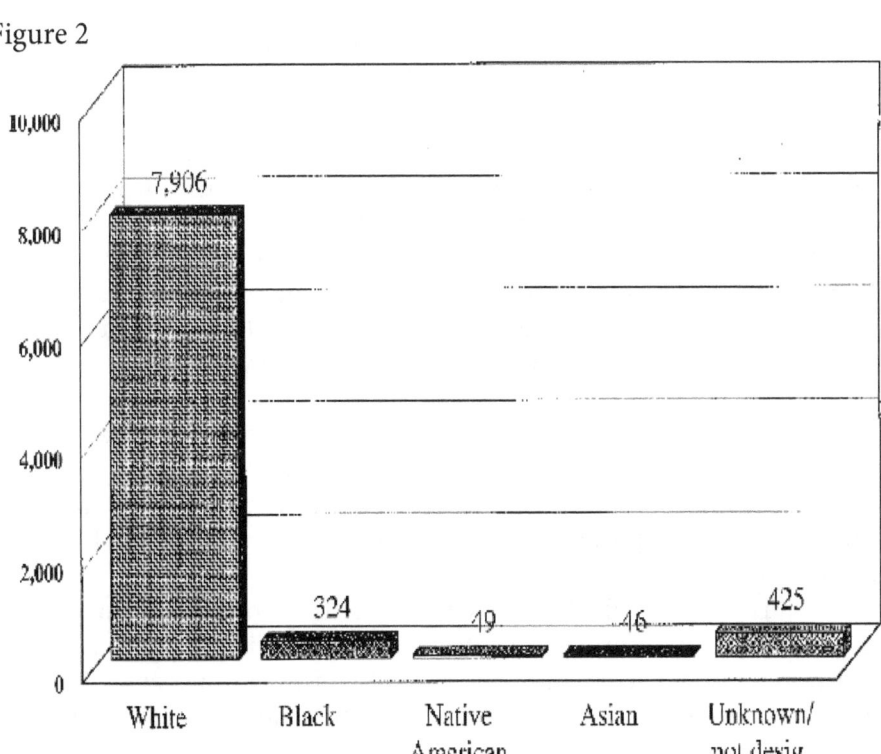

Source: Vermont Department of Corrections snapshot database June 30th, 2011. Persons with multiple statuses are counted only once.

*Reproduced with permission from the Vermont Department of Corrections

moved him and his brother to Vermont. Jankowski says there was "one time when I was little, I was like 13 or 14, I was in Massachusetts and I took some liquor and ran out of the store." The crime that landed Jankowski in jail the first time was for selling drugs "I was selling it on the side to make money." He admits that he transitioned to stealing later on because of the harsher consequences for selling drugs.

Only at the end of our interview did Jankowski open up to me about his family life. Suffering from alcoholism Jankowski's mother was unable to take care of him and his brother. Knowing the state would take them away, Adam made it a priority to take care of his younger sibling and stopped going to school so he could stay home.

To explain where socioeconomic discrimination begins, I would have to write the stories of the millions of individuals who have served time throughout history. These stories are too many to tell in one book, each one filled with a never ending cycle of circumstances that landed someone in jail. The following scenario is a combination of the life-styles of the inmates I spoke to.

"Jerry" was born in Winooski, a small town outside the most populated city in Vermont. Made up of a hardworking, 85 percent white population, money is a constant struggle for the average family. Jerry lives with his parents and his younger brother in a small house on Main Street, a block from the local school.

Jerry spends his days playing with his friends, going to school, and dreaming of becoming a professional fighter like the ones he sees on TV. His mother works at the local Rite Aid stocking shelves and working the register as his father does construction and the occasional odd job.

When Jerry turns 13 his father packs up his things and leaves their family. As Jerry watches his mother cry he makes a promise to her that it'll be okay and that he will take care of them. His mothers works more hours now coming home from work at eleven, she leaves at seven in the morning. Jerry looks forward to the day he'll be old enough to get a job so he can make some money and help his mom out.
Three years go by and Jerry see's his father about twice a year. He's now 16 and a student at the high school.

One night Jerry picks up his little brother at school and once home, they prepare a snack of cookies. He realizes there's no milk as his little brother starts to cry, refusing to eat the cookies unless he can have a glass of milk. Looking in his coat pocket Jerry has no money and his mother doesn't come home for hours. His brother begins to scream demanding milk. Jerry grabs his coat and his brother's arm and pulls him outside as they begin walking towards the corner store.

Outside the store Jerry turns to his brother and tells him to wait for him outside. He walks into the store and makes his way to the back section grabbing a small pint of milk. He sticks it underneath his jacket with his hands in his pocket. He walks out the store smiling at the cashier on his way out. His brother is outside and asks why he didn't get the milk? Jerry looks at him and tells him he did but he had to steal it because he had no money. "I'm going to pay for it when I can get some money" he says.

They begin their walk home until a police car stops in front of them, blue lights flashing. The officer walks out and asks Jerry to hand him the milk and get into his car. Jerry listens and holding his brother's hand, he climbs into the backseat of the police vehicle. Once at the police station the officer calls his mother and asks her to come and pick them up. Once she gets there she yells at Jerry for stealing telling him. "It was a stupid thing to do," she says.

Now whenever Jerry walks down the street the police cars stop and ask him where he's going. They know his name and what he looks like. One day there's a robbery at the local pharmacy and a police car stops Jerry and asks him where he was that evening. Once he believes Jerry wasn't near the pharmacy he leaves. This is not the last time Jerry gets stopped by an officer, it starts to happen all the time.

When one of Jerry's friends gets his license they drive around the "rich" neighborhoods banging down mailboxes for fun. Jerry doesn't ever participate but he drives around with them in the car. This is what Jerry and his friends do for fun because going to the movies is too expensive and shopping for things they can't buy is no fun. Jerry's group of friends is growing bigger; some of them are older and invite him to their parties. One of his friends asks him if he'd be willing to sell some marijuana for him at the high school. Anything he sells he can keep a portion of the money. Jerry likes the idea of having money so he can help out his mom and get himself some new clothes.

At the high school Jerry makes a hundred dollars in an afternoon. He makes a promise to himself that he won't do it again but for Jerry, it's too late. Police arrive at his house and arrest him. One mistake has taken Jerry's life down a new path he will never manage to escape.

Jerry's mother is unable to afford a private lawyer for him and his father is not reachable. On the day of his arraignment Jerry meets his assigned lawyer while a boy his same age as Jerry is also waiting outside and is met by a private lawyer Jerry recognizes from TV commercials. Jerry asks the young man what he did and finds out they have both committed the same crime.

When in front of the judge Jerry apologizes and promises he will never do it again. It's too late and he is sentenced to nine months in jail. The young man with the private lawyer is sentenced to do community service for four months. Jerry doesn't understand how the same crime receive such drastically different sentencings? Was it the judges' bias? Was it the different lawyers?

This scenario may be fictional but unfortunately it is occurring every day throughout the American criminal justice system. Jerry will serve his time in jail and then be released only to be faced with his one mistake for the rest of his life. Jerry won't attend college because he can't get a scholarship. Finding a job will be difficult because many places won't hire ex-convicts. His mother struggles to pay the bills as Jerry watches his family slip into despair. Without a job Jerry has no choice but to repeat the mistake he made when he was 13. He begins stealing TVs' and selling them. He is arrested three more times in the next ten years.

Jerry's life is a hypothetical character created out of the lives of the inmates I spoke to. For some of them, their lives didn't take the wrong turn as early as Jerry's while others were already providing for themselves by the age of thirteen. Each story of theirs is diverse but the pattern that is formed remains the same. A pattern of poverty, judgment, and the struggle to escape a life of imprisonment.

For inmate Adam Jankowski, his childhood was far from traditional. With a single working mother, Jankowski had to look after his brother. "I had to take care of him so he didn't get taken by the state and they actually took me" said Jankowski. "I helped by my sacrifice, helped him live a different life" he said. After the first time he was arrested Jankowski's mother sobered up and has not had a drink since. Francis's and Jankowski's stories are just two examples of the many stories of first crimes individuals from a lower economic class commit. All the other inmates I spoke to had a history of difficult childhoods with absent parents and drug or alcohol abuse. The crimes committed by these individuals were all before the age of 18 and mark the beginning of their continuous time incarcerated.

Photo by Ashley Aubert
The courtyard at Northwest Correctional Facility

Chapter 2

You Have the Right to an Attorney, One That you Can Afford

Photo By Ashley Aubert

The location of meetings between inmates and their attorneys.

Francis and Jankowski were both represented by public defenders assigned to them for the price of around 25 dollars. Public defenders are a topic of much discussion when it comes to socioeconomic
status and incarceration. The idea of hiring someone for a small price
comes with the notion that the lawyer hired is not as adequate as a
lawyer that would cost a lot.

As public lawyers assigned by Vermont Andrew Gilbertson and
Brian Dodge process cases from individuals who cannot afford private
representation. Created in 1963 the Supreme Court created the law
that every individual no matter how poor would have legal representation. Because of the quantity of cases they handle, most public defenders are not able to meet with their clients before their first court appearance. The amount of cases to be processed is simply too many and too
frequent.

The inmates I spoke to felt that having a private lawyer would
have increased their chances of getting a lower sentence simply because of the extra time a private attorney is able to spend with their
clients. Dodge has about 70-80 cases on average and has had up to 125
in his case load. "They feel desperate, very unsupported" said Dodge
who believes there's a lack of help for people from lower economic
levels "The answer is to arrest everybody he said."There's less societal
involvement and understanding and trying to help people."

The stereotypical image of the public defender as a young
twenty something year old straight out of law school does not relate to
the public defender I spoke to. Sitting behind their desks piles of cases
lie on the floor next to them, on shelves behind them, and on empty
chairs. The attorneys I spoke to admitted to the downside of having so
many cases but it was never apparent that this affected the quality of
their work.

Coworker Andrew Gilbertson explained how in situations
involving drug addictions, a person from a high economic status can
go to rehab. Telling a judge you are going to attend a rehabilitation
program will help your chances. For individuals lacking money, rehab
is expensive and rarely affordable. Not being able to get the help they
need means they are more likely to get into trouble with drugs again
said Gilbertson.

According to Matthew Valerio, Defender General of Vermont,
85 percent of the cases in Criminal Court are represented by the public

defense system. They represent almost 100 percent of the people in juvenile court. "Socioeconomics is probably the largest driving factor in the criminal justice system," said Valerio.

In the past forty years, the public defense system has not seen a significant change in the amount of representation, despite the fact that crime in general is decreasing. The question remains, is there a solution to the large percent of low income individuals being arrested even with the crime rate decreasing? "There's no evidence, despite efforts over forty years that it is fixable. Could we manage it better? Sure" said Valerio.

Jeffrey H. Reiman, author of the book The Rich Get Richer, the Poor Get Prison states two reasons an individual with money is more likely to receive a shorter sentence. The first is the fact that a rich individual can afford to post bail which may send the idea out to the public that they are innocent. If the case goes to trial, the jury may have opinions on the defendants guilt before they are presented with the necessary evidence. A poor individual who cant afford to post bail will have to stay incarcerated until they have to appear in court. The second reason as I have previously mentioned is the ability of a rich person to afford private representation who will have more time to dedicate to the individuals case.

Inmate Jankowski had strong opinions on the influence money can have in terms of representation. "You can buy freedom. It's not who you are, it's who you know" he said. If you have money you can buy a lesser sentence because you're paying your lawyer to find a technicality of some sort, he said. "If I had more money I would be able to buy my way out of it, out of the severe consequences." Jankowski has been represented by public defenders in the past but for his most recent arrest, he was assigned a private lawyer for the price of 25 dollars because of a conflict of interest. He feels that had he not gotten private representation, he'd be serving more time than his estimated one year sentence.

Dan Davies, an employee at the Northwestern Correctional Facility also has strong opinions on the role of money in finding a lawyer. "Somebody coming from a well known family that has money on the side who can afford an attorney that will assist them through the system, they are more likely to get a lesser sentence then those guys that come from welfare families, the harder parts of town and are assigned a public defender" he said.

Photo By Ashley Aubert

The entrance to the Northwestern State Correctional grounds.

Chapter 3

Tough Transitions

Photo By Ashley Aubert

Recidivism is the likelihood an individual will be incarcerated again once they are released from prison. As shown in figure 3 Vermont 50.2 percent of women will return to prison compared to 52.3 percent of men. Recidivism is a growing issue in American society; it is proof that a solution to mass incarceration does not exist. Being released is a scary thought for many inmates because they know of the challenges they are going to have to face from finding a residence, to a job, and seeing family and old friends. Before an inmate is released they must have an approved resident where they can live.

For Michael Francis finding a residence has been his biggest struggle."It's all up to me" he said. Francis has called family, friends, and distant relatives to ask if he can stay with them but his main concern remains if he will ever find an approved place to live. If he had $500 dollars to pay to stay at one resident he's found he could maybe even be released early. Inmates who find appropriate living conditions are sometimes released earlier then their actual release date. Unfortunately Francis doesn't have the money and will have to wait until his release date when he hopes he will have somewhere to go. Preferably, he says, he would like to get out of Vermont and travel south to Florida.

Finding a job can be especially challenging for people with a record. Many places don't hire convicted felons while other companies who say they do not discriminate, will find a reason to not hire someone who has a record. For Francis, yard work or construction is what he hopes to do when he is released. Compared to some of the other inmates I spoke to Francis didn't seem that worried. "There's work out there, just gotta find it" he said. Due to a large increase in inmates over the age of 50, the transition back into society has become an added struggle. Figure 4 displays the dramatic increase since 1977.

In the book *It's about Time, Americas Imprisonment Binge*, James Austin and John Irwin outline the many difficulties individuals being released from prison have to endure. From a psychological point of view getting back into the real world can be a shock to the system as the inmates will have been used to a very slow paced lifestyle. Comparing the transition to that of a young white male trying to find a job and a place to live the challenges are even bigger for inmates.

Many state prisons provide inmates being released with a small amount of money to aid them in the transition. The amount of money is never enough and does not last long. According to Austin and Irwin some inmates have jobs while incarcerated earning less than minimum wage and will have saved up for when they are released, others will re-

Recidivism- % of Released Inmates, male and female, reconvicted within 3 years of being released.

Figure 3

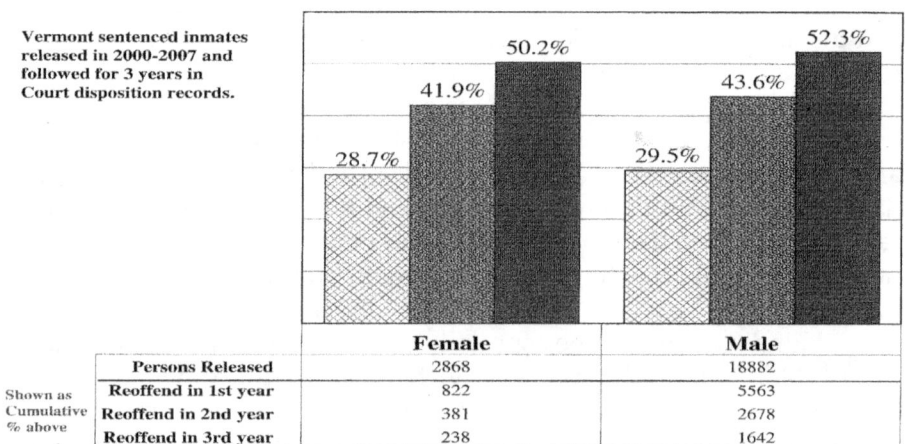

	Female	Male
Persons Released	2868	18882
Reoffend in 1st year	822	5563
Reoffend in 2nd year	381	2678
Reoffend in 3rd year	238	1642

Source: Vermont Department of Corrections (VTDOC) Daily Snapshots and Vermont Court Disposition (in loaded to VTDOC for probable matches.)

*Reproduced with permission from the Vermont Department of Corrections

ceive funding from family members. Figure 6 shows the overall criminal activity committed by individuals on probation.

In the book *Marked, Race, Crime, and Finding Work in an Era of Mass Incarceration,* Devah Pager outlines reasons individuals released from prison should be able to get employed. A primary reason is the fact that an individual who is employed will be much less likely to be involved in criminal activity along with being less likely to take part in criminal activity in the community. From the point of view of tax payers the cost of keeping an inmate incarcerated is far higher than an individual out of prison. Although these reasons for employing ex inmates may make sense, the fact remains that finding employment is next to impossible. From a study by the Oxford University Press it was found that between 75 and 80 percent of individuals on parole were still jobless a year after having been released.

According to Pager the reasons employers may have for not hiring ex inmates are not all based on the idea of hiring a "convict." For some employers, inmates are lazy and generally do not want to do any work or if they have the desire to do work, they don't have the skills. Another reason is the change that individuals go through while incarcerated that may make an individual less suitable for the present day job. Long periods of time spent not doing work may affect the skills an inmate once had. On the other hand, being incarcerated can affect the way an individual interacts with others and forms relationships that may affect their ability to hold down a job.

In states such as New York, Hawaii and Wisconsin, a certain amount of protection is given to former inmates. An employer may ask a prospective employee if they have a record but can only choose not to hire that individual if the crime they committed could have an effect on the job they are applying for.

For Adam Jankowski the transition back into society is not of great concern. He is not worried about seeing old friends with whom he used to be criminally involved. I don't associate with people that are in here he said, and outside "ll pretend to put the number in my phone, I don't associate with anybody that has anything to do with any type of crime." As for finding a job, Adam doesn't mind if he has to work a job most people wouldn't choose. He looks forward to getting out, "I'll work at McDonalds; I just wanna be with my family now" he said.

While "on escape" in Florida Jankowski stole items such as $50,000 worth of jewelry, thousands of DVDs, and lap tops. Because he was on escape Jankowski couldn't get a job as that would have entailed giving them his social security number. Since I was on escape, they

Inmates 50 years of age or older

Figure 4

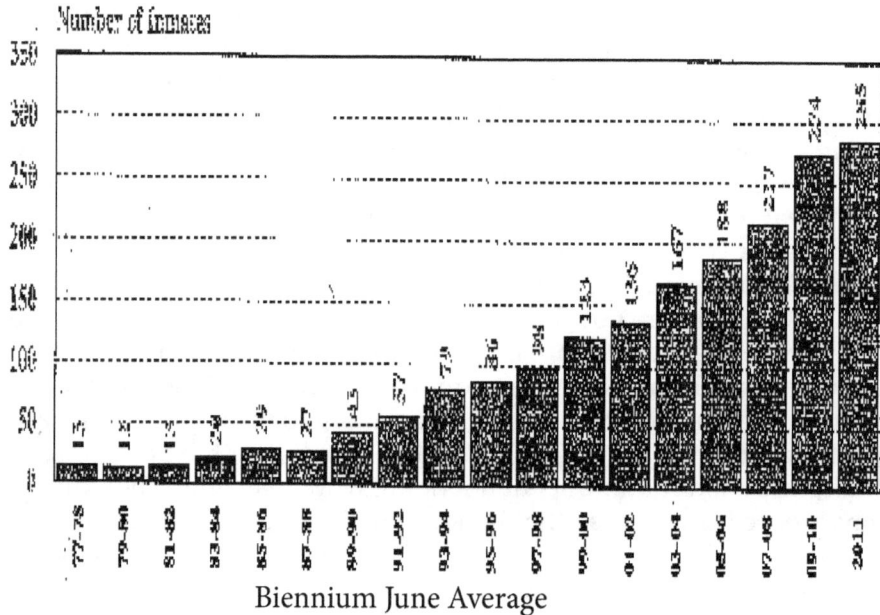

Biennium June Average

Source: Vermont Department of Corrections quarterly profiles (June 1989-1999) and Daily Snapshot (2000 and thereafter) from June 30th. Earlier years from various population reports. Note:: 1977-1996 include housed (incarcerated), on escape,and on furlough. Thereafter the count includes incarceration only.

*Reproduced with permission from the Vermont Department of Corrections

would have found me using that. To earn money he began stealing "that's what brought me here now" he said.

For women, the transition back into society is just as difficult. Pam Greene is the mentoring coordinator at Vermont Works for Women, the first and only organization in Vermont that helps women released from jail transition back into society. The organization says Greene came about because when asked what would help them become more successful once they were released, female inmates would say "we want a buddy, we want one trustworthy friend" said Greene.

For so many of these woman, their families have betrayed them completely "they have to totally start over" said Greene. According to Greene the women who choose to have their own mentor and actively participate in building a relationship with these people are 80 percent less likely to return to prison. The recidivism rate in general has been cut by 80 percent for the women in the program according to Greene.

While doing my research, I noticed how frequently the inmates would vow they wouldn't come back to jail. With recidivism rates being so high, these statements don't seem to hold up. Throughout my interviews with these inmates I grew to understand their characters. It would be untrue to say that I did not worry these men would return to jail after each interview I made sure to tell them they could make it out in the real world if they kept thinking positive and tried their hardest. Today I hope the best for all of them.

Parole, Probation, and FSU

Many inmates once released are put on probation where they are assigned a probation officer and must follow certain conditions assigned to them by the courts. Individuals who are on parole are serving the remainder of their sentence outside of prison and must also follow strict rules. Inmates who violate parole or probation face going back to prison. Shown in figure 5 is the large increase in individuals currently on parole or probation.

Community Corrections District Manager of the Probation and Parole Office in Burlington Vermont, Deb Thibault feels the biggest challenges for inmates is following the rules of parole and probation even though "all they need to do is abide by the conditions of the probation" said Thibault. Most of the individuals who have committed low end crimes never return to prison, while others have a chip on their shoulder and feel they shouldn't have to pay the fines or some don't want to go to rehab to get help for their addictions she said. "We are trying to say come on, just go get this assessment, do what you need to do, open your eyes, just consider it" said Thibault.

One of the primary concerns in parole and probation is drug addiction said Thibault. "By the time we see a lot of young men and women start to come into the system it really is a lot of drug addiction" she said. And because of the large amount of people trying to get help the rehab facilities have a six month waiting list to even enter the facilities she said. For women, the issue goes even deeper because they will frequently have a lot of mental health issues that then coincide with substance abuse.

Another difference between men and women according to Thibault is that women are more likely to want to get the issue resolved right away. "Once the process starts they just want to get it resolved" she said, while men frequently want to fight the charges. Maybe the women should try to fight the charges more? Said Thibault. A lot of times they have children and they're single so it's challenging for them to do.

Contrasting with the inmates I spoke to, Thibault feels that finding a job is one of the biggest struggles for inmates. "Let's face it, if you've got a cashier position open are you going to want to hire someone with retail theft charges?" Probably not she said. Employers and even landlords may look at these individuals differently and you can't lie about having been incarcerated said Thibault.

"Every day's day got to be a challenge for them" said Thibault. "Even if they want to make a change I just think it's hard to come back out into your family dynamics and into that neighborhood or community that you've always grown up and try to make a change there" she said. Despite the negatives, Thibault feels that "if a person is really ready for change and wants support….and they want to apply themselves and are motivated, I do think that given Vermont is so small, that does happen for people" she said.

The strictest form of supervision is FSU or Field Supervision Unit, where officers check in without warning on individuals released from prison. The people who are usually under FSU supervision are considered high-risk and include sex and domestic abuse offenders, gangmembers, and other individuals who have committed a large quantity of crimes. The checkups may occur at the individual's job, at their homes on any day, and may involve random drug tests.

"It's basically on the street but there's a group of like corrections Officers...they come your house, they breathalyze you, they can do searches, they can make you strip…there's really nothing you can hide" said Jankowski who has been on FSU since he was nineteen. In FSU you need to tell your supervisor where you're going to be and when you're going to be there two weeks in advance. You even have to tell them when you're going to have to stop to get gas he said.

"FSU is hard for me, I think for any person. Unless you have a life changing event I would say it's almost impossible because you have to make these passes for two weeks" said Jankowski. Breaking the rules on FSU can be as bad as escaping from jail and can send you back to jail until you serve the maximum sentence for the crime you committed he said. Sometimes you just want to get out, "it's not always that I'm going partying it's not like I'm going to sniff cocaine and shoot drugs and that" he said. "It's hard to walk in a perfect line like that."

PERSONAL INFORMATION
SOCIAL SECURITY NUMBER:_____

LAST NAME:_____
FIRST NAME:_____
MI:_____
ADDRESS:_____CITY:_____STATE:_____ZIP:_____
HM PHONE:_____CELL PHONE: _____MESSAGE PHONE:_____

Are you eligible to work in the United States? YES_____NO_____

If you are under age 18, do you have an employment/age certificate?YES_____NO__

Have you been convicted of or plead no contest to a felony within the last five years?YES_____NO_____ If Yes, please explain:

Growth in Parole and Probation

Figure 5

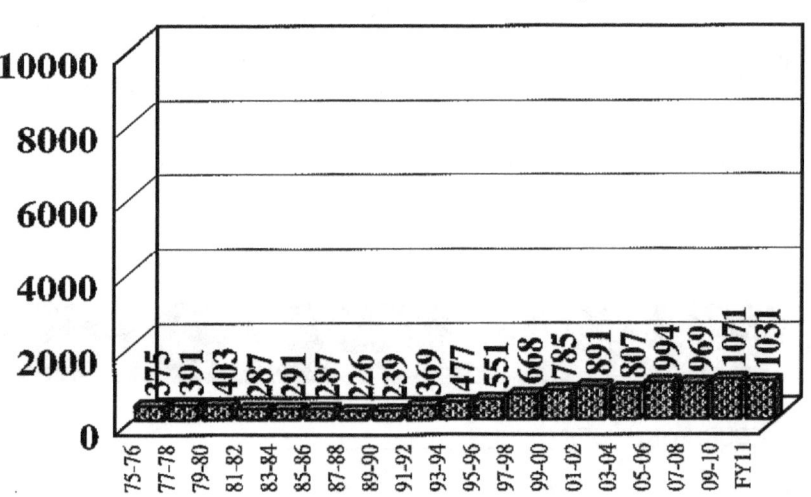

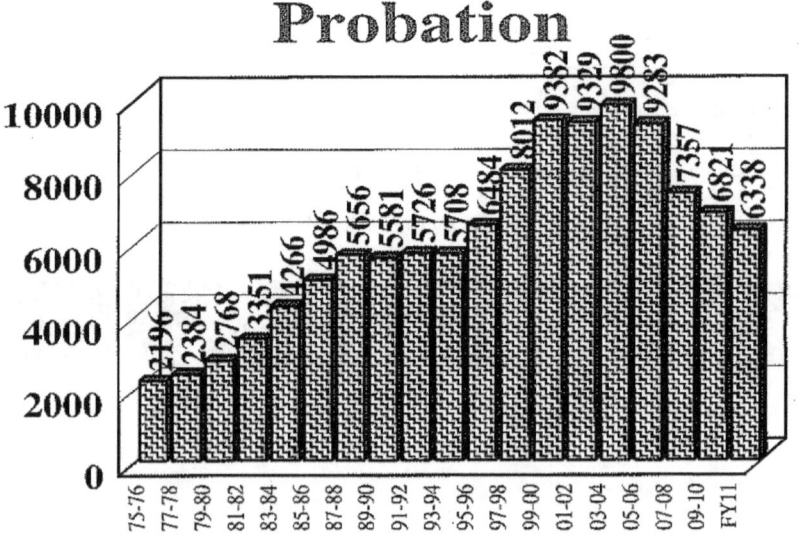

Violation Rates by Probation Type 2011

Figure 6

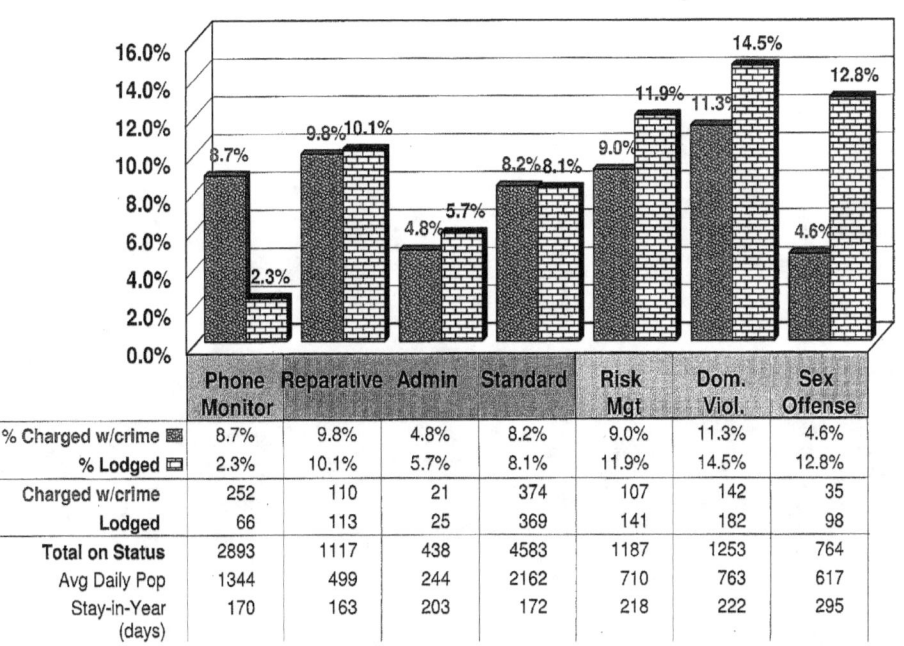

	Phone Monitor	Reparative	Admin	Standard	Risk Mgt	Dom. Viol.	Sex Offense
% Charged w/crime	8.7%	9.8%	4.8%	8.2%	9.0%	11.3%	4.6%
% Lodged	2.3%	10.1%	5.7%	8.1%	11.9%	14.5%	12.8%
Charged w/crime	252	110	21	374	107	142	35
Lodged	66	113	25	369	141	182	98
Total on Status	2893	1117	438	4583	1187	1253	764
Avg Daily Pop	1344	499	244	2162	710	763	617
Stay-in-Year (days)	170	163	203	172	218	222	295

Source: VTDOC Booking and Snapshot database and VT Court filing data (included for probable matching to VTDOC offender identities.) Court filing data received as of October 2011 was analyzed by the fate of the offense (occurring in FY2011) and might not yet completely represent all such charges for the fiscal year which will eventually be filed. The "Total on Status" is an unique count of persons who had at least one day during FY2011 of field supervision at the specified status.

Chapter 4
Meet the Inmates

Northwest State Correctional Facility. Swanton, Vermont

Photo By Ashley Aubert

As the third largest facility in Vermont, Northwest State Correctional Facility in Swanton holds inmates currently serving sentences ranging from 30 hours, to life. The facility is well kept, a large contrast to the media portrayals of dirty, bug infested prisons. Cream colored tiles line the hallways illuminated by fluorescent bulbs reminiscent of hospital rooms. "Please secure the door behind you" signs border each door separated by a small highway. The door can only be opened once the door behind it is closed explains my tour guide. Once inside I notice an inmate getting his hair shaved in one room as another inmate sweeps the floor in the "main lobby."

Built in 1968 the facility originally had only forty beds. Today it holds 250 beds and in the past has reached an all time high of 260 beds. Northwest State holds the largest amount of high risk offenders with different wings separating inmates by behavior. "A" wing holds the individuals with mental problems, the weaker inmates, and the new comers. My "tour guide" explains how men will be placed here at first to see how they handle their new situation and from there may be moved to other wings. Wings "B" and "C" are considered "the zoo" with a hectic atmosphere and no individual bathrooms, there is only a communal rest room that all the inmates must share. Peering through the glass window an inmate taking a shower behind a small door waves to me.

At Northwest Delta, or what is commonly known as "the hole" cells hold inmates 23 out of 24 hours a day. The inmates held here are considered extremely dangerous and very high risk. Although the inmates are separated by wings the dining hall presents what can be a risky situation where the inmates mix together. Fourteen tables each with four chairs make the dining hall look like the lunch room in a school. A sign on the door outside reads "Catholic Mass. Friday 6:30-8:00."

There is a sense of attempted normalcy in this facility equipped with a library, educational building, and a gym. The facility offers computer classes, auto mechanic courses, and even resume writing lessons. Going through each room the occasional inmate is present but never looks up. In the library a young man appearing to be barely eighteen does a written assignment as an older gentleman nearby reads the paper. It is difficult to not greet them but orders were given before entering the facility to not speak or respond to any inmates. This presented a challenge to me as I was so used to interviewing inmates one on one. The no contact rule didn't stop many of the inmates from speaking to

Photo By Ashley Aubert

The Community High school of Vermont building on the Northwest State Correctional Facility grounds.

me as I walked past. Inmates peered through cell bars hollering phrases I couldn't understand.

Due to Vermont being so small most of the men in prisons know or have heard of other inmates. Sometimes through relative's marriage or in a particular case a father and son are incarcerated together. For women this can be an issue because the acquaintances are more personal to them. Many times they share a father to their child or frequently may have been lovers while incarcerated. For men being in proximity to someone they know while incarcerated is not an issue while for women, it can become of concern.

One of the largest issues at Northwest State is the smuggling in of drugs. Women are primarily who bring in the drugs as they can carry them in body cavities. For men, explains my tour guide, this isn't as simple as the opportunity to hide drugs in a body cavity is limited. Only when it is a danger to the women or her child, if she is pregnant, for example can officers search body cavities. For men the process is less then pleasing. They will be placed in a cell with a bathroom long enough for them to dispose of any drugs they may have been holding.

The percentage of inmates considered unable to function without medication on a regular basis is at an all time high. The facility used to employ eight full time mental health workers but today there are only two. The reason for this large decrease is a lack of funding. To incarcerate one individual in Vermont it costs 125 dollars a day compared to incarcerating an individual out of state which costs 45 dollars a day. All together the cost of running the facility is about ten million dollars every year.

Meeting inmates has always been of great interest to me and writing this book gave me the opportunity to meet with a variety of different men from very different backgrounds. My decision not to meet with female inmates was originally based on my idea that women in the criminal justice system bring up a whole other array of issues. The reasons they are incarcerated differ completely from men and the topic of my book would have taken a different route. "Men act out and women act in" said Pam Greene, coordinator of a Vermont program that helps women transition back into society once they are released from jail.

According to Greene there are four pathways to crime for women in Vermont. "Childhood sex abuse, untreated trauma, addictions, and poverty." For women from middle classes, the problems are sometimes worse because they're better at hiding it said Greene. In the

Photo By Ashley Aubert

A room in the Community High school of Vermont building.

mentoring program 90 percent of the women are non violent offenders and a large number of their crimes are drug related. "They have a lot of pain and so they start self medicating by using drugs at a very young age."

It has been documented that for women, the pathway to crimes involving drugs is commonly initiated by an older male partner. The reason the men are frequently older is because the women themselves may have never had a father figure present. "If you don't have a job and you don't have an education, how are you going to survive?" Said Greene. Whether it's conscious or not is questionable says Greene but women will deliberately become pregnant to have a man take care of them.

The drugs come into the picture when the women see their partner using drugs recreationally and don't realize that drugs affect women differently. "Women being on the average smaller.... get addicted so fast and they get addicted at very small levels of hard drugs" said Greene. They can get addicted after doing a drug once and the addiction is so bad they'll do anything to get high said Greene. These severe drug addictions become evident in court settings. "They get themselves so down in a downward spiral before they show up at court and at that point they have so much work to do, I mean now they are totally addicted, they have serious mental health issues, their facing serious criminal charges" said Greene. The future can look especially dark for these women.

When it comes to self esteem these women have no confidence "they hate themselves, they have absolutely zero self esteem, they have a lot of self loathing "said Greene. "They don't feel they're worthy of anything and it's because of how they've been treated all their life." These women are their own worst critics she said. They feel like they are no longer a part of society and its programs like mentoring that can help them get their self esteem back and begin to feel like they play a role in the community.

In Vermont the crime of forging checks is especially common for women. Once the women are addicted to drugs they frequently run out of money. They still have to feed their children so they forge checks to feed their addiction and provide for their families. "The problem with women in corrections is that they have kids" said Greene, and the fathers usually don't have custody.

"When your mother goes to jail, there goes everything, your housing, your security, your nurturer and the children are often taken

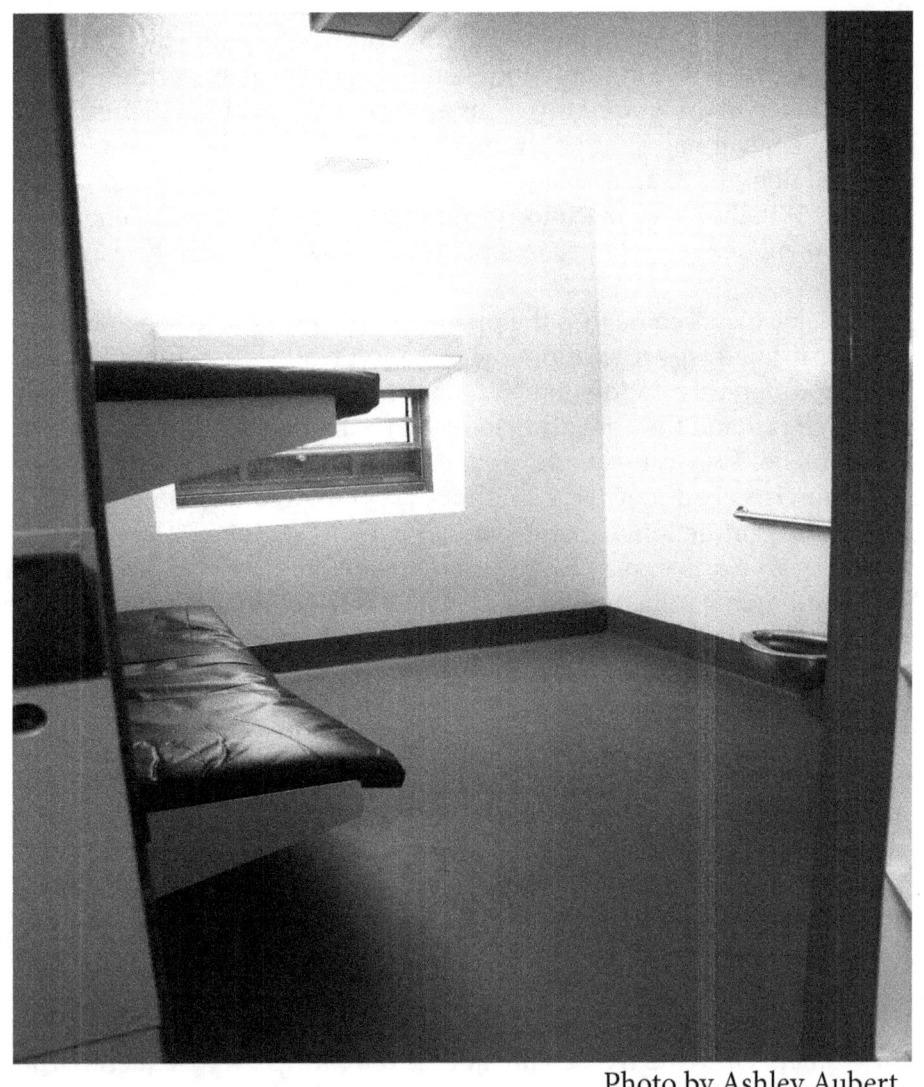

Photo by Ashley Aubert

A cell in the Northwest State Correctional Facility

in by the state, they have to go to foster care and the whole process starts all over again" said Greene. The children feel abandoned and the repercussions of having your mother go to jail are worse than having your father in jail. Greene feels there is a "macho" sentiment when a father is incarcerated but when it's your mother it's like you're wearing a Scarlet Letter she said.

These incarcerated men and women live every day waking up at the same time, doing the same things, and going to sleep at the same time. The hustle and bustle of society is only a far away dream for them. The Chittenden Correctional Center for women is just outside the populated Burlington downtown. Around the corner from a Denny's with a kids "fun store" across the street, CCC is placed in an area you would not expect. The Northwest State Correctional Facility for men is situated next to the small town of St. Albans. A long road surrounded by fields and the occasional house is a strong contrast to the busy downtown area. When I first drove there, I couldn't find the facility and neither could my GPS system which had lost any signal. Only when I looked out to the fields did I notice a building surrounded by barbed wire fences, finally, I thought, I had found it.

Waiting for the inmates I was going to interview I felt a wave of anxiety. These are inmates, I told myself. People who have committed crimes, people who are constantly supervised everyday of their life, these people are desperate. My safety with the inmates has always been a main preoccupation of people and employees around me but for me, it was never the biggest concern. When I visited jail for the first time to interview an inmate I was eighteen and terrified. Sensing my fear an inmate came up to me and said, you are the safest person in here right now, if anyone bothers you…you let us know and we'll take care of them.

When Michael Francis walked in I thought he looked like someone that would be a friend's father. He had sweet eyes and a constant smirk on his face surrounded by graying hair. Originally having a hard exterior shell, only after our second interview did Francis seem to feel comfortable around me. Before that, it was a struggle to get answers out of him that were not one or two words.

At 51 years old Francis has spent most of his life in and out of jail for different crimes. As I mentioned earlier in my book, Francis was alone at the age of 13 and began stealing as a means of survival. When he became addicted to alcohol and opiates he continued stealing as a way to feed his addiction.

After his last release from prison Francis underwent surgery to remove his gallbladder "I keeled over a couple times....couldn't breathe and what not" he said non chalantly. After the surgery his doctor prescribed him medication to which he became addicted again. After he couldn't afford to treat his addiction, Francis began stealing and is now serving time for it. Figure 7 shows the individuals currently incarcerated with histories of drug abuse. With eight grandchildren, Francis' release date in June 2012 couldn't come any sooner. He plans on staying out of jail for good this time "hopefully get a good job, spend some time with my kids and my grand kids"he said.

When I asked Francis what he felt was a primary reason people are incarcerated, he took a while to answer and then said the friends an individual associates with are critical. The police also recognize certain faces he said. Whenever he would go out "they know I've been in a few fights so they'd call in the troops" he said.

An avid fighter Francis admitted to getting into physical altercations especially when alcohol or drugs were involved. As for discrimination against ones class, "by past they treat me differently" he said but many times its appropriate said Francis.

In jail Francis enjoys watching TV shows such as Storage Wars and Scared Straight, a show featuring at risk adolescents who are brought to different correctional facilities to show them what life behind bars is really like. Francis and I shared the same taste for the TV show Lock Up. Ironically, the show tells the everyday stories of the lives of inmates from facilities around the United States.

Jeff Robtoy first went to jail when he was 15. Growing up in St. Albans, he has been in and out of jail his whole life. Today he is serving his 54th day for a crime he claims he never committed, "If I had a real lawyer..." he begins explaining how he feels having a public defender is why he is serving time for a crime he allegedly did not commit. "Drinking, drugs, and girls" says Robtoy admitting that was all it was ever about. Today Robtoy says he is with a girl who doesn't do drugs and doesn't drink. They still keep in contact while Robtoy serves his sentence.

According to Robtoy the main reason someone from a lower socioeconomic level is incarcerated is because they are not able to hire a private lawyer. "No buts about it" he says, it's most definitely the lawyers office. According to Robtoy, if his public defender had sent him a letter informing him of the date he should appear in court he would have never gotten into trouble in the first place.

Prior Drug Use of Jail Inmates , by Type of Drug 2002 and 1996

Figure 7

	Percent of jail inmates who used drugs							
	All inmates				Convicted inmates[a]			
					In the month before the offense		At the time of the offense	
	Ever		Regularly[b]					
Type of drug	2002	1996	2002	1996	2002	1996	2002	1996
Any drug	82.2%	82.4%	68.7%	64.2%	54.6%	54.0%	28.8%	34.9%
Marijuana or hashish	75.7%	78.2%	58.5%	54.9	37.5%	36.0%	13.6%	18.0%
Cocaine or crack	48.1	50.4	30.9	31.0	20.7	22.8	10.6	14.3
Heroin/opiates	20.7	23.9	12.0	11.8	7.8	7.9	4.1	5.1
Depressants[c]	21.6	29.9	10.7	10.4	6.1	5.3	2.4	2.2
Stimulants[d]	27.8	33.6	17.1	16.5	11.4	9.6	5.2	5.6
Hallucinogens[e]	32.4	32.2	13.4	10.5	5.9	4.2	1.6	1.4
Inhalants	12.7	16.8	4.2	4.8	1.0	0.9	0.2	0.3

a) Includes all inmates with a current conviction or a prior conviction but no conviction for the current charges.

b) Used drugs for at least once a week for at least a month.

c) Depressants include barbiturates, tranquilizers, and quaaludes.

d) Stimulants include amphetamines and methamphetamines.

e) Hallucinogens include LSD, Ecstasy, and PCP.

*Reproduced with permission from the Vermont Department of Corrections

Of the inmates I spoke to, the youngest inmate was 19 year old Levi Burleson currently serving a seven month sentence. Originally from Buffalo New York, Burleson feels Vermont is harsher when it comes to crime. "They know I went and destroyed twenty seven cars" said Burleson "I get drunk and get stupid." Burleson was risking serving a 5-25 year sentence but feels because a relative paid for a private lawyer he got only one year instead.

The police know who you are so they are more apt to see you. "People build their own reputation" he said. Appearance also plays a big role in an individual's likelihood of getting arrested he said. Showing respect for the court is important so not showing up in sweatpants and a T-shirt is crucial. Burleson looks like a young man in his twenties and admits that looking older has helped him. If he hadn't been able to get into clubs, things would have been different he said. Being released in May 2012 Levi's father and younger brother are also currently incarcerated.

Adam Jankowski has always felt he stood out in Vermont. In part because he is black but according to Jankowski the way he dresses and the way he talks played into making him stand out from the day he moved to Vermont from New York. Six feet tall with dark skin and bright green eyes Jankowski has an exotic look rarely seen in Vermont. "Where I'm from things are different" he said. "Were louder, flashier. Here its slowed down so when I come I stand out" he said.

When I went to high school people automatically thought I played basketball because I'm black he said. They would automatically think I could dunk. Even buying things for friends was a new experience. "I'll buy everybody something to drink with food stamps, like… that's cool. Out here, they're like oh you get food stamps? You're poor." Being treated differently followed Jankowski onto the streets. I've had people accuse me of doing things that I've never done he said.

"I've had people say that they know it was me" to have stolen something said Jankowski. People coming up to me asking me where they can find drugs when I wasn't even involved in that stuff he said. "I get stopped all the time, where's the weed at or where's the coke at? Like I'm supposed to know just because "he said. People would say "he knows where the weed at" even though at the time, I wasn't selling drugs and I had a job.

While he was in New York Jankowski had never considered himself as being different. If you took a poll of people from New York who were incarcerated in Vermont, they would tell you that not even a year had gone by since their move to Vermont before they got arrested said Jankowski, and that arrest would be the first time they get in trouble, they would have no record, nothing he said.

"I wasn't one that stood out in the crowd where I'm from, I was just an average person, but then I come up here and I'm outspoken....." he said. "People don't act the same from different places." Moving from a city atmosphere to rural Vermont was a huge transition said Jankowski.

When Jankowski began selling drugs for money he says people began recognizing him. "Where I'm from there's always competing. Somebody's trying to be number one and I was never number one where I'm from, but then I came out here and people made me feel like I was number one."

Throughout our interview Jankowski hinted at the fact that he always felt he has missed out on a piece of his childhood because he was incarcerated so young. "I was locked up (from the age of 15-18) so I felt like a part of my childhood was taken away. A lot of things I missed out on like prom and the whole high school experience" said Jankowski who only went to high school for one year.

Today a lot of Jankowski's friends have families and their own businesses which Jankowski hopes to have some day. Describing his younger brother, Jankowski said he hasn't had a problem fitting in. He has a Mohawk thing and wears those skater shoes he said. Just 16 years old Jankowski's brother already has plans to go to college.

Growing up there was always a feeling of not being able to catch up with everyone. "I felt like I was behind them, why am I so far behind all the other people and there the same age as me. I should be right up there with them and I'm not even close to owning a house, so now I need to take a short cut to try to catch up to where I was supposed to be at which is what led me to do the drugs and selling drugs to try to get back to where I was supposed to be" he said.

These are the inmates that I was given permission to interview, always with an employee in the room. There was never a glass window separating us, only a table. Wanting to know about the prison population as a whole I requested information on the hundreds of other inmates behind bars I wasn't allowed to speak to. The ones that were not willing and the ones that were simply too dangerous.

Dan Davies, an employee at NWSC for more than 20 years has noticed a drastic change in the inmates. There used to be respect both ways said Davies. Today the inmates are all so different with so many being from out of state "they don't care" he said. There almost seems to be a sentiment of being proud of where they are like they think "I'm in jail, I'm somebody now."

Vermont is the easiest place to be incarcerated according to most of the inmates I spoke to and many of the employees. The Vermont system is much smaller in general so the facilities are less likely to be over capacity. According to Davies, Vermont is considered to be very lenient with its sentencing's. This doesn't mean the inmates are any better behaved Davies explained, "We're getting inner city guys, heavy hitters ten years in reikers island, they know the rules but when they go to the point where the rules don't matter…" Another facility in Newport Vermont witnessed one inmate walk into the lunch hall and carve another inmates' face, just because, said Davies.

Contrary to popular belief, its not the individuals serving life sentences that cause the most problems. Usually they have long term jobs inside the facility and Davies has found that they are trustworthy in most cases. The kids doing six months or more are the problem said Davies. According to Francis, the young inmates are the issue because of the lack of respect they have. Joining into the conversation, Francis told me of a situation in the lunch hall in which a young inmate called him an old man. With a look of anger on his face, Francis explained how difficult it was for him not to attack the inmate.

Photo by Ashley Aubert

The road to Northwestern State Correctional Facility. Swanton, Vermont

Photo by Ashley Aubert

The Northwestern State Correctional Facility

Chapter 5
Tangible Proof

Photo by Ashley Aubert

In my research I came across a pattern whenever I would ask whether socioeconomic level played a role in an individual's criminal history. The inmates rarely pointed to outstanding proof that discrimination was occurring. This was a strong contrast to the professionals I spoke to who felt that especially in Vermont, a person's economic status was a huge player in the criminal justice system.

I began to form an argument that these two different opinions were formed because the individuals most affected by it, those from low economic backgrounds had been witness to the discrimination their whole life. Not knowing any different, society looks dark to those individuals and a chance to get out of the cycle is rare.

A large part of socioeconomic discrimination focuses on physical appearances such as an individual's clothing or the way they wear their clothes. Are police more likely to stop an individual with tattoos who wears his pants too low? Michael Beyor, an employee at Northwestern State Correctional Facility says "I think society in general does look at that stuff. Sadly society's glass is half empty not half full.

I think society looks even if they hope for the best and really want to think the best, they prepare and think the worst and that's sad. It says something about humanity." Whether the Vermont police do in fact judge on appearances is questionable and whether the theory on judging someone's appearance is real or not, "that's perception" said Beyor.

Coworker Dan Davies says there are three factors that when combined with socioeconomic status contribute largely to an individual's likelihood of becoming involved in criminal activity. Mental illness, criminal family history, and drugs and alcohol are huge players said Davies. Not only are these factors harmful to an individual but they make being an active part of society difficult. For a lot of these individuals, they get more money on welfare so they don't see the point of getting a job he said.

Pam Greene uses the term "inter-generational poverty" to describe the issue of poverty and crime. It's a large problem because these individuals have no role models and getting out of what they have seen their whole life in their families and making their own decisions is difficult to break out of.

An individual who doesn't finish high school and doesn't go to college may find a job working for minimum wage which doesn't solve the problem."You cannot live on minimum wage" is what I've been told said Greene. When they face such a small chance of surviving because they're living on minimum wage a lot of individuals will figure, maybe I won't even try and just go along with the criminal life said Greene.

Christopher Frappier is an investigator at the public defender's office and has been involved in the criminal justice system for more than 25 years. Frappier has seen his fare share of individuals from low economic backgrounds and feels there is a definite connection between the socioeconomic level of an individual and the criminal justice system.

"It sucks to be poor" said Frappier, what is even worse is being poor with a mental illness and a registered sex offender. Focusing back on socioeconomic status alone, Frappier says history proves there has always been discrimination against the poor. Slavery has been around for centuries and that involved slaves who were very poor.

According to Frappier the law is designed to keep loose ends from causing havoc, the loose ends being the under class. The world of law caters to the "haves," not the "have-nots" and the police are never looking for the "haves." They aren't going to be looking at the members of the country club doing cocaine or the college student dealing drugs because those individuals are the money makers of society said Frappier.

Even something as simple as transportation is constructed for individuals with money he says. In Vermont a lot of people live in rural areas where there isn't any public transportation. The individuals living here who have to get to work will risk getting into more trouble when they drive their cars on a suspended license because they have no other choice.

The Police are more apt to stop a car that is beat up with tape on their windows instead of a really nice brand new car said Frappier. It's not that the police are always doing it on purpose and purposefully looking for the beat up cars it's just that those cars are more noticeable he said. The community's sense of comfort is critical according to Frappier. In a rich community no one is going to want to have an individual dressed poorly with tattoos covering their arms walking around their neighborhood. The law is practically set up to keep the rich and "civil" individuals from becoming like the poor.

This is all occurring because the people in charge are the ones with the power and the money according to Frappier. For poor individuals the norms and expectations of society has a huge effect on them.

Society tells them they are not a human being if they don't have these things, or dress a certain way and with no money they have to steal to feel like they are part of society. "Is it criminal? No" says Frappier, "it's human."

Marcus Cambiano practiced law from 1980 to 2000 and has represented the most individuals sentenced to death at one time in history. In 1989, Cambiano represented one of Americas largest mass murderers, Ronald Jean Simmons sentenced to death after murdering his whole family. Working as a private lawyer Cambiano also did pro bono work that included some of the execution cases.

In large trials prosecutors are frequently elected officials and have a lot of public pressure on them to prosecute a crime that has outraged society. Along with the police department Cambiano says they will try their hardest to prove that a person is guilty even if they are not. For a person from a low socioeconomic level they have public representation which does not promise them a lawyer that will be adequate to go up against the prosecution team.

Deb Thibault also says poverty has a lot to do with crime. A lot of people think these individuals have a lack of education and that has something to do with it says Thibault but, for a lot of inmates women especially, they have their high school diplomas. The problem arises when they are single mothers and getting employment becomes a struggle because they need to stay at home and take care of their children.

The issues of poverty are rooted much deeper. "It's more about living in poverty and what they see around them, how they're basically brought up" says Thibault. If you don't have money you might not be able to continue your education and get a better job and it becomes a kind of downward spiral. Maybe they won't have transportation to get to their jobs and they also don't have the means or the support even if they wanted it. The neighborhood a child is raised in is crucial according to Thibault. If a couple has to work all the time and isn't able to stay at home to watch their children a lot of the time they have people from the neighborhood baby-sit. If you live in a bad area, that's not good says Thibault.

For an individual using drugs, they may be getting into trouble but it can be difficult for the police to charge them. "Those kinds of individuals sometimes come into the criminal justice system because the community doesn't know what to do with them anymore." The police are sick of getting phone calls from their family or friends. What they really need is mental help instead of the authority telling them what to do said Thibault.

Dave Turner is the superintendent at the Chittenden Correctional Center for women. There's a large difference in the attitude of the police when they are in a rougher neighborhood said Turner. "They are always on the lookout" and individuals from low socioeconomic levels will be treated differently whether it's because of how they dress, smell, or even how they speak.

I think it's a problem he says, and the police should try to suspend their judgment. In Vermont the neighborhoods are much smaller along with the number of police. I can't even imagine what it's like for people living in the inner city where there are more problems and a lot more police said Turner.

Turner explained how he and his wife have been telling their children they will attend college since they were little, it's become a kind of second nature. Turner asks what families from poor neighborhoods tell their kids? Do they constantly warn their children "stay away from the police?" asks Turner. Could warning their children of the police as being threats represent second nature to individuals from low economic statuses?

Professor Gwen Jordan has been teaching law and criminal justice classes and has studied how socioeconomic status relate to the criminal justice system. According to Jordan socioeconomic status is at the center of how the criminal justice system operates with a list of factors being especially detrimental to individuals lacking money. One factor stems from the kinds of behaviors we label as criminal that are frequently targeting poor people according to Jordan. We might think a crime someone with money commits is "immoral" but rarely do we consider these crimes to be really criminal and rarely are they prosecuted let alone punished.

A second factor is the representation an individual without money may receive. A lot of times public defenders don't have the staff or the resources and are overwhelmed said Jordan. Another factor is considering what exactly brings an individual to commit a crime, what are the causes and why are they being committed?

"People who grow up in neighborhoods where there isn't a good education system and there aren't strong systems of support, there aren't jobs or job training, are going to end up trying to make their way in non legitimate means because legitimate means are not available to them."

According to Jordan the police play a large role in socioeconomic discrimination. There are drugs in all economic classes but the police go to the poor neighborhoods said Jordan. They are specifically choosing poorer neighborhoods and going to search there for drugs.

"Part of that is from the incentives that they get based on the federal government, they give out grants to different police departments to engage in certain kinds of behavior, military will provide certain kinds of services to police departments across the country if they're engaged in certain kinds of activities." Most of the people in high positions in the criminal justice system go after the people who are the most vulnerable in society.

Using a large city as an example, Jordan says when you take a large portion of the black men from a neighborhood, you're taking away fathers and other important people who help make the neighborhoods work. People then ask where are all the young black men? "Well, they're all in prison, they can't be there to take care of their families" says Jordan.

This means there are more single women trying to provide for their families. "Children are the fastest growing group that's living in poverty and that just perpetuates that cycle" says Jordan. If your father is incarcerated and your mother is underpaid what options do you have? Said Jordan.

The people in power are trying to keep wealthy white men at the highest point on the hierarchy says Jordan. "They are the politically connected wealthy primarily white primarily males in our society that are making these decisions, they are making them in their own interest so they can maintain their power." These people want to keep the poor people at the lowest level of the ladder. "They don't want real equality" says Jordan and today our society is not moving towards equality.

Even the plea bargaining system is geared towards people pleading guilty to a felony. A lot of the time an individual will plead guilty and bargain with the courts even though they did not commit the crime in the first place. When an individual weighs the consequences of going to trial and serving a longer sentence if found guilty, they compare it to if they plead guilty right away and serve less time.

The second option will look like a better idea. A lot of the time individuals don't know the consequences of having a felony even if you don't serve time. "That's the way that our system is set up. It's not just money but a whole web of policies and problems that an individual is going to face."

Photo by Ashley Aubert

Chapter 6

Literature Review

Photo by Ashley Aubert

A window looking out into the outside area of the facility.

Author of the book *The Rich get Richer and The Poor Get Prison* Jeffrey H. Reiman starts off his argument by stating that prisons may serve more as training grounds for further criminal activity rather than rehabilitative facilities. In my research I have come to believe that the crimes most frequently sentenced to the most time are more frequently committed by poor individuals. These crimes include burglary and selling drugs.

A rich person charged with embezzlement will not receive the same sentence as a poor young man charged with burglary. When looking at these two crimes one can see that the crime committed by the rich individual is far worse. For example, a successful business embezzles 50 thousand dollars while a person from a poor neighborhood robs 500 dollars worth of jewelry in a break-in. How is it that the rich individual will receive less time than the poor individual?

In a sample proposal, Reiman asked his students to imagine a society where crime is committed by a certain *class* of individuals that are born into criminal activity. What would this class and the individuals in it look like? The responses he got are a perfect example of where and what the problem is in today's society. The students began by outlining crimes that would be considered illegal, many of which really are illegal in the real world.

The fact that crimes such as prostitution are illegal in many ways makes no sense as there is no immediate victim in prostitution. Only when prostitutes have abusive and controlling pimps is there a victim. Second, by the time an individual is incarcerated the students said they would know of another individual who committed the same crime but got less time to serve or no time at all.

Third, Reiman says his students described the overall experience of being incarcerated as painful, demeaning, and all together harmful to people. Fourth, this class of people who are at this point, inmates, would learn no valuable skills while incarcerated but instead, spend their days in their cells sleeping or talking with others.

Last, these inmates would be constantly reminded of their past. With no chance of ever starting a new chapter they would be deprived of a good job because of their past and looked down on by the rest of society. The sad ending to this proposal according to Reiman is that the description his students gave of what this "class of inmates" would look like is obviously very unfair, but an accurate portrayal of the current reality that is the criminal justice system in America.

In a report released by the Report and Recommendations of the

Governor's Commission on Corrections Overcrowding an outline of recommendations on how to effectively reduce the amount of individuals in correctional facilities around Vermont is given. According to the report the current state of overcapacity and "the current corrections system is destructive of human potential and fiscally unsustainable." (Department of Corrections Response, Page 1)

The first recommendation by the Department of Corrections is to make use of global positioning systems for prisoners. Through the use of supervision of released offenders in the community assurance of public safety would remain a priority while decreasing the demand for incarceration. It is estimated that about ten individuals will be involved in the program at any time which would mean ten beds in a correctional facility are vacated. As for a time period in which the GPS would be used, the report states that after 90-180 days of GPS tracking, the inmates would be released once they have proven to be ready for a lower level of supervision.

One of the concerns in using tracking for offenders released into the community is the amount of scrutiny that is frequently put on the offenders. This, according to the report is found to increase incarceration instead of reducing it. The report recommended speeding the process in which individuals currently on probation are held under detention. Although many individuals found to be violating probation are not detained, those that are detained are frequently incarcerated and held without bail. This results in additional bed space being used.

The next recommendation featured in the report is to end the incarceration of individuals going through detoxification. Due to the fact individuals incarcerated for intoxication have usually not committed a crime it goes against the role of correctional facilities which is to protect the public and punish offenders. Individuals who have not committed a crime and are not a threat to themselves or those around them should not be incarcerated according to the report.

Along with not being a threat is the fact that correctional facilities do not have appropriate medical requirements for an individual detoxing and "the staff are not trained or accountable for the degree of expertise necessary for these persons." Along with this is the fact that individuals not charged with a crime can only be held for a maximum of 24 hours and therefor incarcerating these individuals is pointless and could be harmful to the health of those requiring medical aid.

Discharging those that are ready to be discharged from correctional facilities is critical in the efforts to reduce incarceration rates. According to the report, at any given time there are one hundred inmates who have completed all requirements yet do not have approvable housing. I was able to see this first hand with inmate Michael Francis who could have been released any day but could not find appropriate housing and was therefore forced to wait until his release date in the next months.

In an effort to help resolve this issue the proposal of centers for inmates about to be released was offered as a means of transitioning offenders who are awaiting housing. The issue in question is where to build these facilities that could present potential problems for the surrounding communities. A recommendation was made of using the grounds of correctional facilities around Vermont to build the centers. In a response released in 2006, the Department of Corrections made a statement that they would work with the Department of Buildings and General services in hopes of creating a possible plan. Today, housing for the released offender still remains a primary concern.

A critical recommendation is the necessity for continued support for inmates searching for housing and employment. Both of these were reoccurring issues in the interviews I conducted with the inmates. The report recommended removing the obstacles that are presented to inmates seeking housing and employment once they are released. These obstacles to be removed include the establishment of free telephone calls and free postage stamps for offenders while still incarcerated.

Other recommendations offered by the report include improving the process in which sentences are calculated to which the Corrections Department responded by stating that the calculations involved in sentencing are complex. A recommendation also offered was to help lower the rate of incarcerated women by offering alternatives. This is based on statistical research that shows the rate of incarcerated women has been increasing more than twice as much as men. Another factor in the rate of incarceration of women is the non-violent offenses that the majority of women are currently serving time for.

On the topic of parole and probation, the report recommends eliminating the collection of fees owed by offenders and reviewing the whole probation system in part because of the large increase in the amount of parole and probation cases. Giving judges the authority to place an offender on work crew as a means of paying off fees that are due. As a conclusion the report recommends reviewing the parole and probation system as a whole to which the Department of Corrections responded they would review the system but would have to wait for the results from other strategies put in place in the hopes of decreasing the inmate population.

After reviewing the report it would seem that the Vermont Department of Corrections did not follow through with the recommendations. Written in 2005 Vermont's prisons are still increasing in inmate population, whether the inmates are returning on new charges or a simple unpaid fine. It is difficult not to question whether the incarceration system as a whole has become an area of little hope for change. It is unlikely that the Department look over the recommendations and act upon them, I feel it would be beneficial to all individuals involved in the justice system and would allow Vermont as a whole to be an example for the rest of the country.

So, how do we understand how this problem in American society is caused? According to Reiman, there are already many excuses in existence such as the "urbanization" of modern life and the simple excuse that we just don't know how to reduce crime. Reiman does admit that urbanization may contribute slightly to an increase in crime but in no way does it deserve all the credit for our current situation. He gives examples of small cities where the crime rate is lower than large rural areas.

The other excuse that we simply do not know how to reduce crime is even more inaccurate. Reiman says we know some of the causes of crime such as poverty, yet we aren't making any drastic changes to stop poverty in America. With the recent Occupy Wall Street movement, we can see that Reimans thoughts (written in 1984 in this particular book) are still very relevant to our present time. Obviously, the issues have not been resolved.

The way to understand socioeconomic disproportionality in the American criminal justice system is by looking at the "failures" as Americas successes. Reiman proposes that criminal justice policy wants to maintain the current level of crime instead of reducing it, otherwise...wouldn't we already have fixed it? The reason this would be happening goes back to the idea that those in power seek to maintain their positions in power.

The current imbalance in the criminal justice system is beneficial to those with money, remember the business man who embezzles 50 thousand and gets a short sentence? Reimans argument is that the current justice system is protective of those with power and lets face it, why should those in power have to preoccupy themselves with poor people?

Starting off with when an individual is arrested Reiman collected research evidence that proved the likelihood of a rich individual

$ Wealthy White-Collar Criminals $

$ Walter J. Ratliff- Former Texas state senator charged with embezzling state funds.

Received six months in prison, two years' probation.

$ Seymour R.Thaler- Elected to the Supreme Court of New York. Shortly after he was charged with having received and transported $800,000 worth of stolen Us Treasury bills.

Received one year in prison. Had to pay a $10,000 fine.

$ Jack L. Clark-President/Chairman of the Four Seasons Nursing Centers altered reports and earnings projections as a means of inflating his stock. Shareholders lost an estimated $200 million dollars.

Received one year in prison.

$ Valdemar H. Madis-At the time was a wealthy drug manufacturer. Diluted an antidote for poisoned children with a fake "copy" substance.

Received one year of probation and was ordered to pay a $10,000 fine.

being arrested for a crime was lower than for a poor individual. In a study done by Ronald Goldfarb.[1]

"48.2 percent of juveniles arrested in California were released by the police after some informal handling and without charges being preferred, but in the upper middle class suburban community of Lafayette in Contra Costa County, 80 percent were released after arrests. Of the total juveniles arrested in California, 46.5 percent were referred to a juvenile court; in Lafayette, 17.9 percent. Of those who eventually were institutionalized, the California average was 5.3 percent; in Lafayette County,1.3 percent." (Reiman, page 83)

Although this research statistic was done in California, Reimans chapter features numerous examples of different places across America in which this trend reoccurs various times. An explanation for this may lie in the fact that poor people have less privacy, what many people do in their living rooms or backyards, the poor will do out on the street, clearly visible to police officials writes Reiman.

As I mentioned in Chapter one, sentencing varies depending on one's economic status. An individual without money will be assigned a public defender while someone with money will be able to hire private representation. That is not to say that public defenders are not adequate lawyers, the difference lies mainly in the amount of time a private paid lawyer can spend with their client which will help the overall case.

In the third edition of Americas Prison Binge by James Austin and John Irwin the focus is on the dramatic increase in the incarcerated population of the United States and it's ties to socioeconomics. According to Austin and Irwin the "war on drugs" which began in the 1980's played special attention to one drug in particular, crack cocaine. Most commonly sold and used in inner city areas the war on drugs caused a huge increase in the percentage of minorities and poor individuals arrested.

According to Austin and Irwin societies desire to get rid of individuals in society who are a bother to the rest is what has created an even larger gap between the rich and poor in America. With increasing incarceration populations come increased costs and less money spent combating poverty, drug abuse, and crime. It is the desire to feel safe that has cause the public to demand stricter punishment, life sentences for repeat offenders, and the death sentence.

---

1   Ronald Goldfarb,Reiman, J. (1984). The Rich Get Richer and The Poor Get Prison: Ideology,Class,and Criminal Justice. (Vol. 2nd Edition, Ed.). Allyn & Bacon.

According to Austin and Irwin most individuals currently incarcerated are non- violent offenders serving time for drug or property crimes. If society wants to feel safer, why are most people in prison nonviolent? Why is the incarcerated population increasing as the overall crime rate decreases? According to Austin and Irwin many believe that these "street criminals" will commit more crimes if they are free. The best way to stop this from happening is to incarcerate all these "street criminals" (proven to be majority nonviolent) and to make sure they are incarcerated for long periods of time. Figure 8 shows the large increase in misdemeanor sentences. A misdemeanor is a crime that does not sentence an individual to a year in prison, unlike a felony which means an individual is sentenced to at least one year for the crime.

One of the primary reasons individuals are being sentenced to longer times in prisons are new laws for re-offending individuals or "habitual offenders." An individual who has committed numerous crimes may be considered a habitual offender and, although the crimes are non-violent they face the possibility of serving a life sentence. The three strikes law is another example in which an individual who commits three or more "serious" crimes may be sentenced to life in prison.

In Vermont an individual who has committed a variety of crimes ranging from murder to aggravated sexual assault a total sum of three times faces the possibility of serving life in prison. In a research statistic involving inmates considered habitual offenders results found that 87 percent of the victims involved in the crimes had suffered no injury. Most of these habitual offenders were categorized as being crack heads with the smallest percentage being drug dealers.

Whether incarceration even reduces crime remains a widely discussed topic. Results show that crime rates are going down and incarceration rates are going up leading to the possibility that perhaps incarceration is helping lower crime rates. From another point of view is the theory that the crime rate is decreasing and the incarceration rate is increasing not because of more people being sentenced but because people are being sentenced for a much longer time. These two results vary among states. Currently, California and Texas show the largest increase in the number of individuals incarcerated.

Austin and Irwin describe ex-inmates as "damaged goods" in that, as hard as they try to lead a normal life the challenges are always there. All the inmates I spoke to had hopes of getting respectable good paying jobs, a good home, and enough money to be able to provide for their families. The sad truth is that the majority of these individuals go into prison without an education, money, or a job and once released, find themselves in that same situation.

Number of Misdemeanor Sentences with Time to Serve as Imposed by the Court

Figure 8

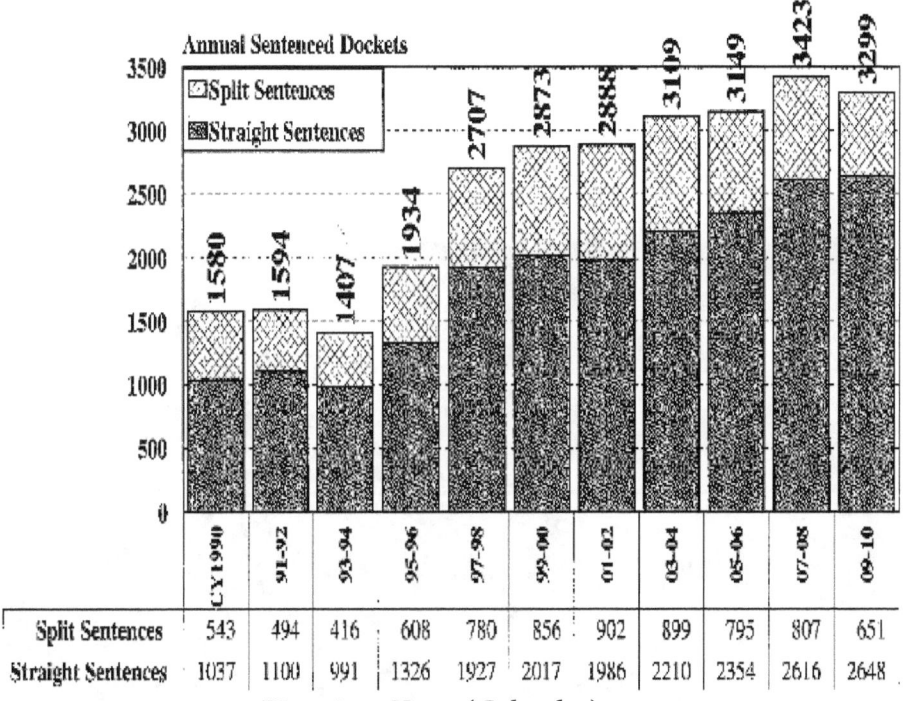

	CY1990	91-92	93-94	95-96	97-98	99-00	01-02	03-04	05-06	07-08	09-10
Split Sentences	543	494	416	608	780	856	902	899	795	807	651
Straight Sentences	1037	1100	991	1326	1927	2017	1986	2210	2354	2616	2648

Biennium Years (Calendar)

Source: Vermont Center for Justice Research, annual updates. Counts of charges/dockets with sentences imposed, NOT persons nor "court cases" involving multiple charges.
Note: "Time to serve" might be served in actual incarceration or under an intermediate Sanction Agreement with supervision in the community.
"Split" sentences are terms of incarceration followed by probation; the offender is not paroled.
"Straight" sentences have minimum and maximum terms: the offender may be released on community reentry program and/or parole.

*Reproduced with permission from the Vermont Department of Corrections

Chapter 7
Solutions

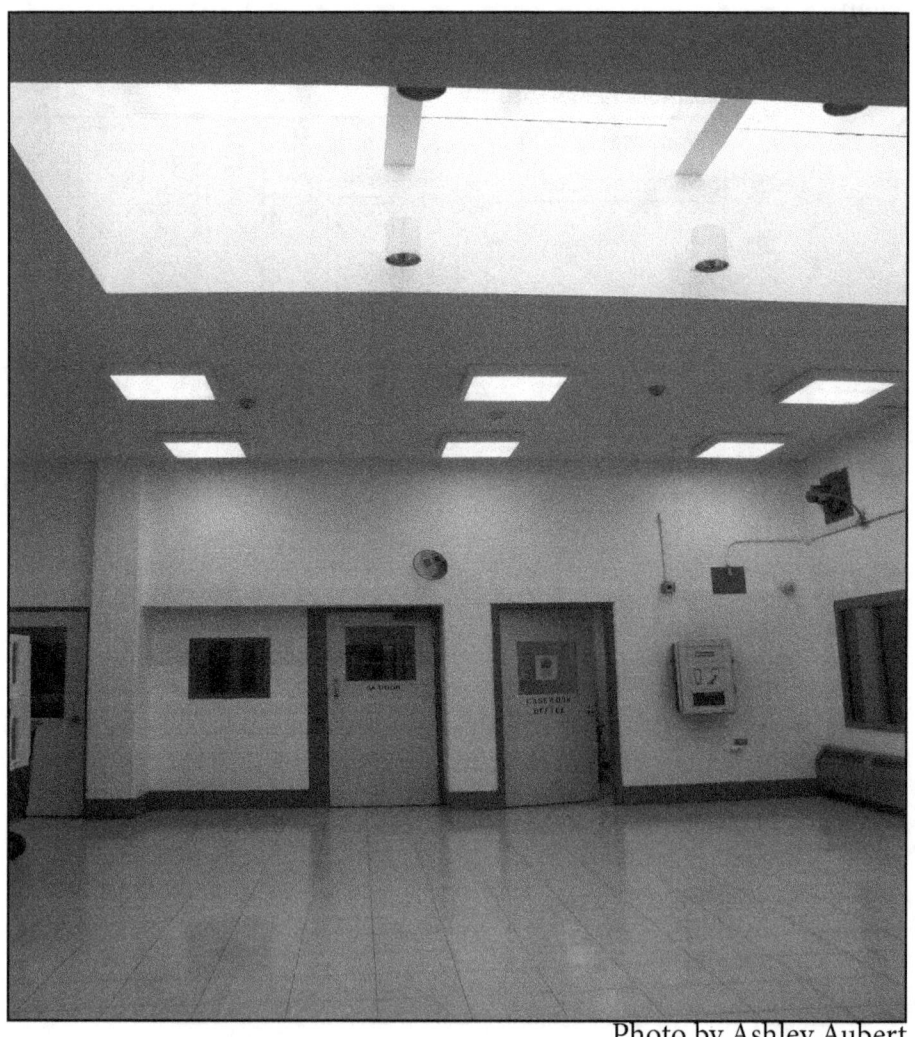

Photo by Ashley Aubert

The lobby inside the facility.

When it comes to an issue like socioeconomic status and incarceration, solutions can seem challenging and even impossible. After conducting numerous interviews, I got a sense that there was really no way of fixing the issue and it was just a part of society. How would America be able to get rid of poverty overall so that discrimination against individuals without money didn't occur? And how would the most powerful individuals, those that many argue are responsible for the discrimination, suddenly change their attitudes and decide to act differently to change society's perceptions as a whole? In Vermont, could jails and prisons be improved as a step towards improving the whole criminal justice system?

Inmate Michael Francis had strong opinions about improving the facilities themselves. According to Francis the young inmates have a lack of respect towards others and each other. When a young inmates breaks the rules the correctional officers will enforce new rules that affect those of us that haven't done anything wrong said Francis. "Just have one system for the kids and one for the adults, cause a lot of the rules they do make are for the kids, yu know a lot of the older guys are just set back" he said

According to Francis, the young inmates are happy in prison. They have their friends here and their parents send them money to keep them out of their hair he said. The parents of these inmates' are happy to because they know where their children are, they know their safe. The current system doesn't make it hard enough said Francis. "Vermont corrections are just easy." For Francis, his grandchildren are what keep him going while he is incarcerated. I wanted to ask him if he worried they would ever end up incarcerated like him. "Hopefully papa or dad would sit down and talk to them" he said smiling, "papa" being Francis himself.

As for the correctional system in general, Francis feels rehabilitation instead of incarceration would be a step in the right direction. Asking me if I've seen the show "scared straight" which features young teens who are at risk sent to prisons around America in hopes of having them change their ways, Francis says Vermont should try a similar program "I've always said it would be a beautiful thing if Vermont had that."

Defender General of Vermont Matthew Valerio is an important individual for any changes in Vermont's incarceration system. How to handle and organize the individuals who commit the crimes is a critical part of any change in Vermonts' criminal justice system. The real question according to Valerio is what kind of people need to be in jail? "There are a lot of different ways we deal with offenders and jails tend to be the place we put them when we don't know what else to do with them" said Valerio. For individuals guilty of non-violent crimes it would make more sense to not just incarcerate them but instead provide them with supervision and support such as rehab and mental health treatment options said Valerio.

The media also plays a huge role in the portrayal of the criminal justice system in Vermont. "I think that the media, politicians and kind of just the general talk on the criminal justice system is very misleading "said Valerio. "We are unbelievably safe in a state like Vermont. Crime rates, particularly regarding violent crimes have been dropping for decades yet people feel less safe than they did 20 years ago or 30 years ago and statistically, they would be much more at risk to be the victim of crime 30 or 40 years ago then they are right now." The all-around access to news whether online, or smart phones, or TV is partly to blame says Valerio. "Whatever it is leads people to believe that we are under siege by criminals when in fact by any statistical measure that is not the case."

According to Deb Thibault, the creation of more half way houses for men and women would be beneficial to Vermont. Similar to Valerio's opinion, Thibault feels less jails and more direct referral to boards (such as parole) would also be an improvement. It's annoying to think that someone charged with checking bad checks is looked at carefully by the police, we need to focus on the people that represent a concern for the public's safety said Thibault.

According to author Jeffrey H. Reiman, the criminal justice system needs to do what it essentially claims to do, protect and do justice. The real dangers that threaten to harm society are what we need to do be protected against according to Reiman. The criminal justice system should not be partners with those that cause injustice in our society.

First off to protect society there must be stringent gun control according to Reiman. Described as a constant temptation to individuals considering committing a crime. Taking away guns would mean the disappearance of the temptation. "Trying to fight crime while allow ing America to remain an armed camp is like trying to teach a child to walk and tripping him each time he stands up" writes Reiman. (Reiman, page 197) Another method is to make producing and buying heroin legal. Although this may seem like a strange method, Reiman backs up his argument saying that rehabilitation for those addicted to drugs is critical.

Reiman even goes as far as proposing that heroin be prescribe-able by doctors for individuals over 18. The reason for this is simple, addicts will commit crimes to obtain drugs. If the drugs are easily obtainable there are no crimes to be committed. There is also the simple fact that heroin, although easily addicting, when taken in appropriate doses, does not present extreme dangers. Of course, offering rehabilitation for individuals addicted to heroin would be crucial.

As for correctional facilities a change must be made within the programs offered to inmate. Personal responsibility is of huge importance according to Reiman and instead of being undermined, it is necessary to train inmates for the real world. Reiman makes the argument that incarcerating "children" is pointless. Once they are released they have learned nothing on how to survive in the real world, it comes of no surprise that inmates like 27 Adam Jankowski who was incarcerated at 15 follow a path of "constant" incarceration. The lack of preparation of young inmates is a violation of the Eighth Amendment against "cruel and unusual punishment" says Reiman. (Reiman, page 201)

For the public to believe that the criminal justice system is trying to protect us, crimes that are harmful to us must be punished. Crimes such as petty theft may be annoying but to say they cause harm to an individual is an exaggeration. Setting clear guidelines on the law is crucial so individuals know the risks when they decide to act in certain ways or do certain things. Crimes with no victims such as gambling, public intoxication, and drug use should not be criminalized says Reiman. Only crimes that cause harm to victims deserve to be punished by the law. This includes white collar crimes which as we have seen, cause harm but are rarely punished to the extent of most victimless crimes.

The second change needed from the criminal justice system is for there to be more overall justice. Crimes should be judged simply for that, the crime, not the individual who committed the crime or what their background, sex, or race is. From a legal standpoint, Reiman argues that lawmakers need to clarify the different methods they use when deciding the crimes to charge an individual with. Charging someone guilty of one crime with numerous little crimes is useless and according to Reiman, a way for prosecutors to trick the defendant into pleading guilty so as to not face worse charges if the case then goes to trial.

Reiman even makes the argument that something as simple as requiring lawyers to outline on paper why they have charged the individual with the charges and why they have picked that certain sentencing for that individual. There should be more background behind why and how lawyers have made the choices in a case would make an improvement. This would aid in decreasing discrimination, another necessary change according to Reiman. Keeping a close eye on the discretion used by judges all the way to lawyers is critical if an increase in fairness is to be seen.

Lastly, the ability of an individual to have legal counsel needs to be specified to having appropriate counsel. This would decrease the amount of expensive lawyers only affordable to those with money and allow individuals with less money to have "appropriate" counsel decreasing the risk that someone will receive non adequate representation. In summarizing the necessary changes to stop discrimination against individuals from lower socioeconomic status, society as a whole needs to narrow the gap between the rich and the poor, social justice must be put into effect.

In the book It's about Time, Americas Imprisonment Binge by James Austin and John Irwin the justice system must stop the forever increasing number of incarcerated individuals. Along with statistics that say incarceration does not stop someone from engaging in criminal activity, Austin and Irwin make the point that the more people we incarcerate the less money we have for education, child care, and other necessary services. Along with harming society, we are also harming a larger percent of individuals who when released back into society struggle to survive on a day to day basis after having spent months or years locked-up.

What is more important according to Austin and Irwin is not trying to fix the criminal justice system but fixing the issues that cause criminality. These include reducing poverty, unemployment, and to provide better health care for the American people. A lack of these things are proven to be causes of criminality in today's society.

In reducing prison terms, crimes that are considered felonies should be decreased in criminality and become misdemeanors which would shorten the sentences of those accused. Along with less felonies and more misdemeanors, Austin and Irwin add to the common argument of less incarceration and more parole and probation. Remember that it's the individuals incarcerated that are serving longer sentences, not necessarily more people being incarcerated. If sentences were shortened and transferred to parole and probation it would lower incarceration rates while providing individuals with ----appropriate supervision.

To conclude, one of the most important changes that are needed in today's criminal justice system is the necessity for better prison conditions. Giving the inmates the opportunity to help themselves and prepare them for the outside world instead of housing people with nothing to do is critical if we are to see any sort of improvement in the system. There needs to be better health care for prisoners, more reha-bilitation options for the ill, and more help for inmates getting ready to be released. Making these small changes in the facilities themselves would prove very beneficial not only for the inmates but for the crimi-nal justice system itself.

Chapter 8
Small Towns, Big City Problems

Photo by Ashley Aubert
The path towards the outside "recreational" area.

It's always surprised people when I told them what my book was about. "Incarceration? You mean prisoners?" This was a common response and one to which I would have to bite my tongue. All I wanted to tell people was that these "prisoners" were in fact, prisoners, but not in the sense they meant. Many of the prisoners incarcerated today are held captive by society, the demands of society, and the discrimination so many are born into.

The inmates I met were never like the ones in the movies. They look like normal people, fathers, mothers, brothers, and sisters. At no time in my many visits to prisons did I meet an individual with tattoos all over his face. I never received a glance that scared me, frankly, I was never scared. Worried, perhaps after all I was a young college student and humans alike can be unpredictable. I can safely say that I have felt in more danger walking on a busy city street in plain daylight then walking down a hallway with cells on either side.

The inmates I interviewed were always polite. I was asking them to share their stories with me, personal ones at times that many people on the "outside" world would find inappropriate or even rude. To these inmates I represented someone who would listen to their stories whether it had anything to do with my book, I listened. This meant more to the inmates than anything else I felt. Being listened to was something they had rarely been accustomed to.

In fact, a majority of my interviews consisted of inmates going on and on about things that were completely off topic, lawyers they didn't like, other inmates they got into fights with but the point was that they were being listened to. This, I felt, was the least I could offer to repay them for their time. I was never allowed to take pictures of the inmates or any of the employees at Northwest Correctional Facility. I made a decision on my first day that if I had been able to take pictures, I would always blur the inmates faces out. I saw it as a sign of respect so readers wouldn't just view them as these men behind bars.

When someone asks me to describe an inmate I never know how to answer. Describe an inmate? That's like asking someone to describe a man or a woman? The fact someone is an inmate does not make them all alike. There is not a type of mammal known as "the inmate." I like to describe prisons as towns with a small population. There are nice people, mean people, religious people, talented people, lazy people, prisons are not occupied with a population of evil killers. In fact, its quite the contrary.

There are many ways in which the incarceration system could be improved. Discrimination on the basis of socioeconomic status has only tapped the surface and remains almost unheard of. People complain about the police or the over population of prisons. What people need to rethink is who the individuals who make up the incarceration system are. Once people begin to hear the stories and histories of inmates from around the country the issue would become apparent, and undoubtedly changes would be made.

My first solution to the issue of discrimination against the poor in the justice system would be to inform the public. Although there may not be many reports specifically on economic discrimination, there are graphs and statistics that once analyzed, show a large gap and an array of injustices. The only way for people to made aware of issues is for them to be brought forward to the public. Wether through public speaking or different forms of media, my hope is that important figures will shed light on the issue to inform people so advances can be made towards a more just system.

The topic of education reoccurred during my research, especially when discussing low economic neighborhoods. It may seem farfetched to connect bad education to individuals' committing crimes and ending up incarcerated but studies have shown that keeping children busy is crucial to keeping them out of trouble. Organizations such as the YMCA are critical especially in neighborhoods with criminal activity as they are a chance for young children and adults to learn and have fun in a safe place. Whether by the government or by town mayors, the implementation of more educational facilities and resources would prove to be very beneficial to younger generations.

With colleges and universities in America being so expensive, it is no wonder that individuals from lower socioeconomic backgrounds rarely even dream of getting the college degrees. How can we act surprised when we hear that the majority of inmates never completed high school. Why should they? We cannot expect individuals to go through school knowing that even if they graduate high school they will not be able to attend college. They don't have the support whether it is financial or emotional. There are cases in which college students have come from rough neighborhoods, but isn't this a sign that there is a problem?

The mere fact that this student has to be pointed out in my opinion points to the problem. It should not be strange for an individual from a poor neighborhood to attend college. If someone has worked hard they should be allowed to continue their education regardless of what economic background they come from. Lowering the cost of higher education would allow more individuals to keep occupied, but most importantly, it would allow them to have hope for a better future and a chance to become what they have always hoped.

From a legal standpoint, I can only make one recommendation which is to make the laws equal. Yes, I am aware that the law prides itself on being "equal" but let's faces it, it is far from being equal. Why are white collar criminals still getting less time than a young boy who sells some marijuana? How is this equal justice? Only when the laws are equal and individuals who have committed a crime are treated equally can we look forward to changes. Only when the rich do not run the world can all people regardless of their income be treated as one.

In my last proposed solution, I would recommend informing people of the law. So many times I hear of peoples cars being searched without permission or without the individual knowing they have a right to say no. The mere mentioning of authority has become a sort of taboo that people fear, its not surprising that individuals, myself included, will do whatever authority tells us to do. After all, they have the power (and the gun) and I have nothing. Individuals should be given information on what is legal and what searches are warranted.

Knowing your rights does not mean you can break the law and then save yourself from getting into trouble. It gives individuals the tools to protect themselves. If you think of what you did today, can you find one thing that is considered "illegal?" Probably. Now do you feel you should be arrested and sentenced for it? Unless you were dealing drugs on a street corner, probably not. Unfortunately its simple crimes that commonly land people in jail because they didn't know the police had no right to search their car.

Its difficult to think of a possible reason socioeconomic status could be so widely important in the criminal justice system. Through my research I came upon statistical, opinion, and even historical reasonings behind it. From the time of slavery all the way to today, individuals living in poverty seem to receive the short end of the stick. According to Plato "narcissism of minor differences" was to blame for many issues throughout history. The definition of the phrase stems from the idea that little differences in the lives of people who are similar are what cause wars to happen. I make the argument that as human beings we are the same, we are born the same and, we die the same.

In my opinion, Plato was correct in saying that similarities, in this care being human, and minor differences, in this case ones economic standing are what cause the problem of socioeconomic discrimination. The desire, for money, in my opinion is to blame not only for the disparity between the rich and the poor but the unequal treatment of people from different economic backgrounds. Perhaps we could argue that history has changed drastically since Platos time but then it would seem that there is hope that one day, individuals rich and poor will be treated equally, both in the criminal justice system and throughout their daily lives.

Photo by Ashley Aubert

Works Cited

Irwin, John. The Jail: Managing the Underclass in American Society. Berkeley: University of California, 1985. Print.

Clark, Christine. "Diversity Initiatives in Higher Education: Multicultural Education as a Tool for Reclaiming Schools Organized as Breeding Grounds for Prisons." Multicultural Education 11.3 (2004): 50-3. Web. "Decriminalizing Poverty." Nation 291.26 (2010): 12-4. Web.

Easterbrook, Gregg. "Run-on Sentencing." New Republic 220.17 (1999): 57-65. Web.

Frost, Ann. "Descriptive Representation for Minority and Immigrant Populations in the War on Drugs." Conference Papers -- Western Political Science Association (2009): 1. Web.

Hudson, B. A. "Race, Crime & Justice." Race, Crime & Justice (1996) Web.

Huggins, Denise Walker, and Catherine L. Coghlan. "Social Stratification and Life Chances: An Interactive Learning Strategy for Criminal Justice Classes." Journal of Criminal Justice Education 15.2 (2004): 413-28. Web.

James, Joy. "States of Confinement: Policing, Detention, & Prisons." States of Confinement: Policing, Detention, & Prisons (2000) Web.

Johnson, Brian. "Racial Disproportionality in Imprisonment Reconsidered: A Reanalysis of Blumstein's Conclusions using Federal Data." Conference Papers -- American Society of Criminology (2007): 1. Web. "JUVENILE DELINQUENCY-- Other Serious Factors Involved." Congressional Digest 33.12 (1954): 292-314. Web.

Mauer, Marc. "Race, Class, and the Development of Criminal Justice Policy." Review of Policy Research 21.1 (2004): 79-92. Web.

Northern Arizona University. Criminal Justice Collective. Investigating Difference: Human and Cultural Relations in Criminal Justice. Upper Saddle River, N.J.: Pearson Prentice Hall, 2009. /z-wcorg/. Web.

Podgor, Ellen S. "The Challenge of White Collar Sentencing." Journal of Criminal Law & Criminology 97.3 (2007): 731-59. Web.

Roberts, Albert R. Critical Issues in Crime and Justice. Thousand Oaks, Calif.: Sage Publications, 2003. /z-wcorg/. Web.

Smith, Laura, Alizah Allen, and Rashidah Bowen. "Expecting the Worst: Exploring the Associations between Poverty and Misbehavior." Journal of Poverty 14.1 (2010): 33-54. Web.

University of, Southern California. "Jurisdiction Site & Sentence Disparity - Executive Summary." Jurisdiction Site & Sentence Disparity - Executive Summary (1985) Web.

Western, Bruce, Punishment and Inequality in America. New York: Russell Sage, 2006. /z-wcorg/. Web.

Wooldredge, John, and Amy Thistlethwaite. "Bi-level Disparities in Court Dispositions for Intimate Assault*." Criminology 42.2 (2004; 2004): 417,417-456. Web.

Reiman, J. (1984). The Rich Get Richer and The Poor Get Prison: Ideology,Class,and Criminal Justice. (Vol. 2nd Edition, Ed.). Allyn & Bacon.

Austin, J, & J. Irwin. (2001). Its About Time, Americas Imprisonment Binge. (Vol. 3rd Edition, Todd. Clear, Ed.). Wadsworth.
Department of Corrections Response to the Report and Recommendations of The Governors Commission on Corrections Overcrowding.

Rep. 6 Feb. 2005. Web. 12 Mar. 2012. <http://corrections.vermont.gov/about/reports/doc-response-overcrowding/view>.

West Memphis Police Department, WMPD.(c.1993)"Damien Echols Mug shot. "Photograph. West Memphis; Arkansas. Retrieved from www.bing.com

Vermont Department of Corrections — Department of Corrections . (n.d.). Vermont Department of Corrections — Department of Corrections . Retrieved April 2, 2012, from http://www.doc.state.vt.us/

Sources

Michael Francis
Deb Thibault
Chris Frappier
Andrew Gilbertson
Adam Jankowski
Pam Greene
Brian Dodge
Dan Davies
Adam Jankowski
Dave Turner
Gwen Jordan
Marcus Cambiano
Matthew Valerio
Jeff Robtoy
Levi Burleson
Michael Beyor

Photo by Ashley Aubert

Photo by Ashley Aubert